What Makes Buildings Special?

by Lana Cruce

Scott Foresman
is an imprint of

PEARSON

Glenview, Illinois • Boston, Massachusetts • Mesa, Arizona
Shoreview, Minnesota • Upper Saddle River, New Jersey

Photographs

Every effort has been made to secure permission and provide appropriate credit for photographic material. The publisher deeply regrets any omission and pledges to correct errors called to its attention in subsequent editions.

Unless otherwise acknowledged, all photographs are the property of Pearson Education, Inc.

Photo locators denoted as follows: Top (T), Center (C), Bottom (B), Left (L), Right (R), Background (Bkgd)

Cover Lolofranceparis/Fotolia; **1** Eric Bechtold/Alamy Images; 3 Medioimages/ Thinkstock; **4** Brad Pict/Fotolia; **5** Eric Bechtold/Alamy Images, Lolofranceparis/Fotolia; **6** trekandshoot/Shutterstock; **7** Monica McCafferty KRT/NewsCom; **8** Raymond Forbes/ Glow Images; **9** Konstantin Povod/Shutterstock, UK Alan King/Alamy; **10** (c)Jade Albert Studio Inc/Getty Images; **11** (c)Royalty-Free/Corbis; **12** Nancy Kennedy/Shutterstock; **13** Monkey Business/Fotolia.

ISBN 13: 978-0-328-39337-4
ISBN 10:   0-328-39337-1

10 11 12 V010 17 16 15 14 13

Wherever people **dwell,** there are buildings. Some buildings are houses. Some buildings are barns. In the city, some buildings are very tall.

Some buildings are plain. Other buildings are special. On these buildings you can see faces, beautiful flowers, and other lovely things carved out of stone. Special buildings can make a neighborhood special, too.

Here is a building with special things on it. This building is in New York City. It is 77 stories high. A story is another word for a floor in a building, so this building has 77 floors.

The building was built by a company that makes cars. If you take a close look at the building, you will **discover** hidden shapes.

What kinds of shapes do you think you will find on this building?

This is the Chrysler building.

The top of the building looks like layers of hubcaps.

There are shapes of cars and car parts on the face of the building. Some people think the rounded parts look like hubcaps. A hubcap is a round cover that fits over the wheel of a car.

Do you see the eagle heads? These shapes were used on the hoods of cars.

5

Here is another building. It has a **gargoyle** on it. Gargoyles are scary-looking stone figures. They were often put on a building to help the rain run off the roof. When it rains, the water runs out of the gargoyle's mouth.

Some people used to believe that gargoyles could scare away bad luck.

Would you like to live in a building that has gargoyles on it?

One famous building where you can see many gargoyles is in Washington, D.C. It is a large church. It took more than 80 years to build this building.

There are many different kinds of stone creatures on this building. You can see strange-looking people, monkeys, fish, dogs, and elephants.

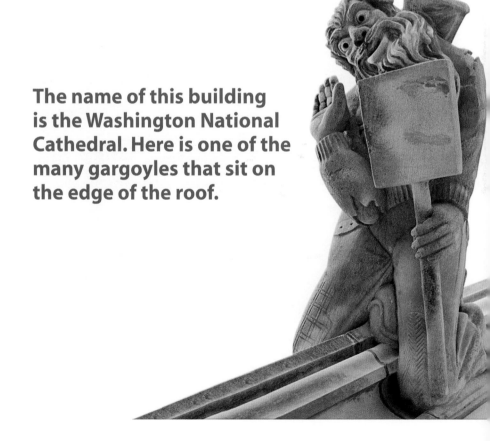

The name of this building is the Washington National Cathedral. Here is one of the many gargoyles that sit on the edge of the roof.

One stone decoration is a **griffin.** This one is on the roof of a museum in Philadelphia. A griffin is a made-up animal. Its front half is an eagle, and its back half is a lion. The griffin is supposed to be very strong and smart.

Why do you think they put a griffin on this building?

**This griffin is on the
Philadelphia Museum of Art.**

Look at the gargoyles on this page.
What do they look like to you?

This gargoyle is in
Oxford, England.

Here is a school building. What special thing do you think would be good for a school building? This school has a picture of the Earth painted on a brick wall. The people who built the school wanted something nice to **welcome** children to the school.

Schools often use friendly figures or pictures to make children feel welcome.

This building shows an eagle on the entrance. Can you guess why? This is a **government** building. You can see a lot of government buildings with eagles. The eagle is our national bird. It is a symbol of courage and strength.

The bald eagle is a symbol of America.

It is not only government buildings that have symbols of the United States. There are barns all over the United States that have our flag painted on them. Have you ever seen a barn or other kind of building that shows our flag?

The owner of this barn is proud to be an American.

Figures and pictures on buildings are all around us. You can see them whether you are a **resident** of a city or just visiting. The next time you are walking around, look up at the buildings. Try to see something you have not seen before. Maybe you will see a face, an animal, or some strange design.

You can find a world of treasures if you just look up.

Now Try This

You have seen and read about many interesting buildings. Now you get to design a building of your own. You will need two pieces of paper, crayons or markers, scissors, and glue.

1. On one piece of paper, draw a building. It could be a house, a barn, a school, a skyscraper, or any other kind of building.

2. On the other piece of paper, draw faces or other things to be on your building. They could be animals, people, objects, or anything you want. Draw things that go best with your building, like the eagle goes with the government building.

3. Cut out the pictures you have drawn.

4. Glue them onto your building, wherever you think they look the best.

Glossary

discover *v.* to find something

dwell *v.* to live somewhere

gargoyle *n.* a creature carved out of stone

government *n.* the people or groups that control a country or state

griffin *n.* a make-believe animal that is half eagle and half lion

resident *n.* one who lives in a certain place

welcome *v.* to happily meet someone